Praying you hear
His **comforting** voice,
feel His **healing** touch,
know His loving **compassion,**
and find your heart at **peace.**

Peace I leave with you. My peace I give to you.
I do not give to you as the world gives.
Don't let your heart be troubled or fearfu
JOHN 14:27 CSB

We want Christ to hurry and calm the storm.
He wants us to find Him in the midst of it first
Beth Moore

DaySpring

May God *comfort* you and, in time, bring *healing* to your heart.

Trust in the LORD with all your heart and do not lean on your own understanding. In all your ways acknowledge Him, and He will make your paths straight.
PROVERBS 3:5–6 NASB

We often can't see what God is doing in our lives, but God sees the whole picture and His plan for us clearly.

Tony Dungy

DaySpring

God's ways so often amaze us—and I'm asking Him to **_amaze you_** today with the **_tender ways He cares for you and your body._**

> Is anyone among you sick? Let him call for the elders of the church, and let them pray over him, anointing him with oil in the name of the Lord. And the prayer of faith will save the sick, and the Lord will raise him up.
>
> **JAMES 5:14–15 NKJV**

Health is not valued till sickness comes.

Thomas Fuller

DaySpring

I'm so thankful that
God hears our prayers.
I'm praying for you with
confidence, trusting
that your healing will be
quick and complete!

*Listen to my voice in the morning, L*ORD*.*
Each morning I bring my requests to
You and wait expectantly.
PSALM 5:3 NLT

God is too good to be unkind and He is too wise to be mistaken. And when we cannot trace His hand, we must trust His heart.

Charles Spurgeon

DaySpring

God's help is **near** and
always available.
May His **healing touch**
be on you today.

I am the LORD, who heals you.
Exodus 15:26 NIV

*Lord, please do this…
or do something better!*
Priscilla Shirer

DaySpring

I'm asking Jesus
to bring you into
His rest today.

Because of the LORD's great love we are not consumed, for His compassions never fail. They are new every morning; great is Your faithfulness.
LAMENTATIONS 3:22–23 NIV

Our hearts can rest peacefully
in the promises of God.

Bonnie Jensen

DaySpring

I'm praying each day that God's blessings will **overflow** in your life—everything **beautiful, healing,** and **strengthening** for your heart, soul, and body.

> Serve the LORD your God, and He will bless your bread and your water. I will remove illnesses from you.
> **EXODUS 23:25 CSB**

Begin to rejoice in the Lord and your bones will flourish like an herb and your cheeks will glow with the bloom of health and freshness. Joy is balm and healing, and if you will but rejoice, God will give power.

A. B. Simpson

DaySpring

Praying that the God of miracles *overwhelms you* with His *incredible goodness.*

For God is greater than our worried hearts and knows more about us than we do ourselves.
I JOHN 3:20 THE MESSAGE

Your name has shown up in the most special places. Your name is written on God's hands. Your name is on His lips.

Max Lucado

DaySpring

Tough times call for **good friends.** I'm here for you and praying you through. **You can count on it.**

Fear not, for I am with you; be not dismayed, for I am your God. I will strengthen you, yes, I will help you, I will uphold you with My righteous right hand.

ISAIAH 41:10 NKJV

Stand firm in the Lord.
Stand firm and let Him fight your battle.
Do not try to fight alone.

Francine Rivers

DaySpring

Whatever you need—
God is. I'm asking
Him to *show up* in all the
ways you *need Him most.*

But the Lord is faithful, who will establish you and guard you from the evil one.
II THESSALONIANS 3:3 NKJV

Faith is the art of falling in love every day with the One who is the same yesterday, today, and forever.

Ann Voskamp

DaySpring

We have a **God of miracles** who parts the seas, feeds the multitudes, calms the storms, and heals our hearts. Praying you'll see Him do ***above and beyond*** what you can even imagine.

But He was pierced for our transgressions, He was crushed for our iniquities; the punishment that brought us peace was on Him, and by His wounds we are healed.
Isaiah 53:5 NIV

How sweet the name of Jesus sounds in a believer's ear! It soothes his sorrows, heals his wounds, and drives away his fear.
John Newton

DaySpring

I'm asking God to give you a *joy so deep* that it will never run out.

Joyful are people of integrity, who follow the instructions of the LORD. Joyful are those who obey His laws and search for Him with all their hearts.
PSALM 119:1–2 NLT

Laugh a little more and it'll hurt a little less.
Beth Moore

DaySpring

I'm praying because ***God hears.***
I'm trusting because ***He cares.***
I'm waiting because ***He answers.***
I'm celebrating because I know that what He has for you is ***so good.***

But I will bring you health and will heal you of your wounds—this is the LORD's declaration....
JEREMIAH 30:17 CSB

This blessed Book brings such life and health and peace, and such an abundance that we should never be poor any more.

Smith Wigglesworth

DaySpring

He sees beyond the here and now to the *healing*, the *hope*, and the *peace*.... *Jesus sees you*—and He's *closer* than anyone could ever be.

This is My command—be strong and courageous! Do not be afraid or discouraged. For the LORD your God is with you wherever you go.
JOSHUA 1:9 NLT

We are secure, not because we hold tightly to Jesus, but because He holds tightly to us.

R. C. Sproul

DaySpring

God has you on **_His mind_** and in **_His healing hands._** I hope you sense His **_love_** and **_my prayers_** today.

> Now see that I, even I, am He, and there is no God besides Me; I kill and I make alive; I wound and I heal; nor is there any who can deliver from My hand.
>
> **DEUTERONOMY 32:39 NKJV**

We are never nearer Christ than when we find ourselves lost in an holy amazement at His unspeakable love.

John Owen

DaySpring

Everyday miracles are God's specialty.

Keeping you in prayer.

You're blessed when you're at the end of your rope. With less of you there is more of God and His rule.
MATTHEW 5:3 THE MESSAGE

Where we find difficulty, we may always expect that a discovery awaits us.

C. S. Lewis

DaySpring

Even when it feels like a lot is broken, ***God can do so much with just a little.*** Stay strong, keep believing— and know that I'm praying often.

I will forgive their sin
and will heal their land.
II Chronicles 7:14 NIV

Earth has no sorrow that heaven cannot heal.
Thomas Moore

DaySpring

I've asked God to give you
all of His very best gifts—
lifting you up, leading you
forward, and *filling you* with
anticipation for what's ahead!

May the God of hope fill you with all joy and peace as you trust in Him, so that you may overflow with hope by the power of the Holy Spirit.
ROMANS 15:13 NIV

We embrace the hand we've been dealt because we know the dealer, and He never deals badly.

John Piper

DaySpring

The arms that fashioned the universe are strong enough to *heal you* and gentle enough to *hold you.* I pray that you find *rest* and *healing* in the arms of our loving Father.

Lord, by such things people live, and in every one of them my spirit finds life; You have restored me to health and let me live.
Isaiah 38:16 CSB

Christ is the Good Physician. There is no disease He cannot heal, no sin He cannot remove, no trouble He cannot help.

James H. Aughey

DaySpring

It might not make sense in the moment, but from the beginning of time, God knew you'd be right here, right now. I've asked Him to *plant seeds of hope* in your heart as you *heal* and *grow* in Him!

There is a time for everything, and a season for every activity under the heavens.
ECCLESIASTES 3:1 NIV

Hope is a seed God plants in our hearts to remind us that there are better things ahead.

Holley Gerth

DaySpring

Today I'm specifically praying that all the ***comforts of God are yours today***—that fear flees, anxiety ambles off, and the peace that passes understanding sustains you in every way.

> I have seen his ways, and will heal him; I will also lead him, and restore comforts to him and to his mourners.
>
> **ISAIAH 57:18 NKJV**

Fear imprisons, faith liberates; fear paralyzes, faith empowers; fear disheartens, faith encourages; fear sickens, faith heals; fear makes useless, faith makes serviceable.

Harry Emerson Fosdick

DaySpring

Just wanted you to
know that you're covered
today by *God's love*
and *my prayers!*

Shout for joy to the LORD, all the earth.
Worship the LORD with gladness;
come before Him with joyful songs.
Know that the LORD is God....
PSALM 100:1–3 NIV

The goodness of God is infinitely
more wonderful than we will
ever be able to comprehend.

A. W. Tozer

DaySpring

I'm praying that the ***God of miracles*** will fill you with ***health and hope***—so much so that it pours out from you to the people around you.

> Nevertheless, I will bring health and healing to it; I will heal My people and will let them enjoy abundant peace and security.
> **Jeremiah 33:6 NIV**

In a futile attempt to erase our past, we deprive the community of our healing gift. If we conceal our wounds out of fear and shame, our inner darkness can neither be illuminated nor become a light for others.
Brennan Manning

DaySpring

In times like these—
there is *peace,* there is *hope,*
there is a *plan,* there is *Jesus.*
Praying for you.

LORD, *be gracious to us! We wait for You.
Be our strength every morning and our
salvation in time of trouble.*
ISAIAH 33:2 CSB

Faith isn't denying our
circumstances. It's believing that
nothing is impossible when we get
God involved in our circumstances and
trust Him through them.

Katie Ferrell

DaySpring

I'm carrying your **needs** daily to the Father in **prayer.**

Dear friend, I pray that you are prospering in every way and are in good health, just as your whole life is going well.

III John 1:2 CSB

The most eloquent prayer is the prayer through hands that heal and bless.

Billy Graham

DaySpring

I'm so thankful that God is the very best Shepherd, *taking our burdens* and *carrying us along the way.* I'm praying you feel that today.

*Come to Me, all you who labor
and are heavy laden,
and I will give you rest.*
MATTHEW 11:28 NKJV

The welfare of sheep depends solely upon the care they get from their shepherd. Therefore, the better the shepherd, the healthier the sheep.

Kay Arthur

DaySpring

It really is a privilege to pray to the **_Creator of the universe,_** the **_King of all kings_** and the **_Lord of all lords,_** just for you.

> And my God shall supply all your need according to His riches in glory by Christ Jesus.
> **PHILIPPIANS 4:19 NKJV**

If you wake up feeling fragile, remember that God is not, and then trust Him to be everything you need today.

C. S. Lewis

DaySpring

My prayers are with you that your *healing will come quickly.*

L%%RD my God, I cried to You for help, and You healed me.
PSALM 30:2 CSB

Affliction brings out graces that cannot be seen in a time of health. It is the treading of the grapes that brings out the sweet juices of the vine; so it is affliction that draws forth submission, weakness from the world, and complete rest in God. Use afflictions while you have them.

Robert Murray M'Cheyne

DaySpring

I'm asking God to **_soothe your broken heart._**

He will wipe every tear from their eyes. There will be no more death or mourning or crying or pain, for the old order of things has passed away.
Revelation 21:4 NIV

They commit themselves to Jehovah-Rophi, the Lord, the Healer, and He either heals their sickness or gives them the grace to endure it.
Charles Spurgeon

DaySpring

Praying that you'll find *strength in the Lord* and in His *mighty power.*

Many are the afflictions of the righteous, but the LORD delivers him out of them all. He guards all his bones; not one of them is broken.
PSALM 34:19–20 NKJV

We are all faced with a series of great opportunities brilliantly disguised as impossible situations.

Chuck Swindoll

DaySpring

Praying God's
wisdom and peace
hold you up and
bring comfort.

Pay attention to my words; listen closely to my sayings.... For they are life to those who find them, and health to one's whole body.

PROVERBS 4:20, 22 CSB

Suffering is part of the human condition, and it comes to us all. The key is how we react to it, either turning away from God in anger and bitterness or growing closer to Him in trust and confidence.

Billy Graham

DaySpring

Praying that the
God of *all abundance*
spares no expense on
your behalf today.

Praise the LORD, my soul, and forget not all His benefits—who forgives all your sins and heals all your diseases, who redeems your life from the pit and crowns you with love and compassion.

PSALM 103:2–4 NIV

The words of kindness
are more healing to a drooping
heart than balm or honey.

Sarah Fielding

DaySpring

I hope you feel **God's love** for you in special ways today, with **healing strength** and **comfort,** chasing all your cares away.

> A merry heart does good, like medicine, but a broken spirit dries the bones.
> **PROVERBS 17:22 NKJV**

True faith means holding nothing back. It means putting every hope in God's fidelity to His promises.

Francis Chan

DaySpring

I'm here for you, praying for you and trusting God for **big things.**

Confess your trespasses to one another, and pray for one another, that you may be healed. The effective, fervent prayer of a righteous man avails much.
James 5:16 NKJV

The thing the church needs most today is the ability to heal wounds and to warm the hearts of the faithful; it needs nearness, proximity.

Pope Francis

DaySpring

May God's *strength* help you move from hurting to *healing* and may God's peace bring *comfort* to your soul.

The LORD will preserve him and keep him alive, and he will be blessed on the earth; You will not deliver him to the will of his enemies.
PSALM 41:2 NKJV

Jesus can heal you everywhere you hurt.

Joyce Meyer

DaySpring

Thinking of you and ***praying*** that God will show Himself **strong** on your behalf.

"He Himself bore our sins" in His body on the cross, so that we might die to sins and live for righteousness; "by His wounds you have been healed."

I PETER 2:24 NIV

Transforming the world happens when people are healed and start investing in other people.

Michael W. Smith

DaySpring

Today I'm asking God to meet you *right where you're at,* with all the *mercy* and *grace* your heart can hold.

God is faithful; He will not let you be tempted beyond what you can bear. But when you are tempted, He will also provide a way out so that you can endure it.

I Corinthians 10:13 NIV

Worrying is arrogant, because God knows what He's doing.

Barbara Cameron

DaySpring

Praying that as you ***give all your worries and cares to God,*** you'll know how much He cares for you.

> Then they cried out to the LORD in their trouble; He saved them from their distress. He sent His Word and healed them.
>
> **PSALM 107:19–20 CSB**

God cares about everything that concerns you, so feel free to talk to Him about anything.

Joyce Meyer

DaySpring

You are capable of so
much more than you know…
in His *strength*…in His *grace*…
in His *love*. My prayer is that you
feel His *courage* in you today!

Freely you have received; freely give.
MATTHEW 10:8 NIV

Live your life from your heart.
Share from your heart. And your
story will touch and heal people's souls.

Melody Beattie

DaySpring

I'm praying that God **holds nothing back for you today**—every need met, every desire fulfilled, every joy complete.

> Our Father in heaven,
> hallowed be Your name.
> Your kingdom come.
> Your will be done on
> earth as it is in heaven.
> **Luke 11:2 NKJV**

Not only has your past been paid for, your future has been provided for.

Joyce Meyer

DaySpring

What's in the name of Jesus?

Joy. Peace. Hope. Love. Humility.

Wholeness. Contentment.

Healing. Rest. Strength. Glory.

The LORD is my shepherd....
He restores my soul.
PSALM 23:1, 3 NKJV

God does not waste an ounce of our pain or a drop of our tears; suffering doesn't come our way for no reason, and He seems especially efficient at using what we endure to mold our character. If we are malleable, He takes our bumps and bruises and shapes them into something beautiful.

Frank Peretti

DaySpring

I'm asking God to show you the size of His ***heart,*** the depth of His ***love,*** and the strength of His ***power.***

It is not the healthy who need a doctor, but the sick. I have not come to call the righteous, but sinners.
Mark 2:17 NIV

Miracles are a retelling in small letters of the very same story that is written across the whole world in letters too large for some of us to see.

C. S. Lewis

DaySpring

Beyond the heartache, the disappointment, and the confusion you're feeling now, *Jesus can see the healing and the hope.* I care about you and am praying for you.

He heals the brokenhearted and bandages their wounds.
PSALM 147:3 CSB

A broken heart heals when we allow the healing to go as deeply as the wound went.

Beth Moore

DaySpring

There's not much I can say,
but there's one thing I can do—
I'm praying for you.
Can't wait to see how God works
all this together for good.

> Jesus continued going around to all the towns
> and villages, teaching in their synagogues,
> preaching the Good News of the kingdom, and
> healing every disease and every sickness.
>
> **MATTHEW 9:35 CSB**

*God grants healing to glorify
the name of Jesus. Let us seek to be healed by
Jesus so that His name may be glorified.*

Andrew Murray

DaySpring

I pray that God will
give you a *peace* today
along with the confidence that
His *strength* will *carry you,*
and His *joy* will *keep you.*

*You have turned for me my mourning
into dancing; You have put off my
sackcloth and clothed me with gladness.*
Psalm 30:11 NKJV

May your sorrow soften gently with time.
May your heart heal gently with love.

Matt Anderson

DaySpring

May Jehovah Rapha,
the God who heals,
strengthen you in
every way today.

For I am the LORD who heals you.
Exodus 15:26 NKJV

Nothing ahead of you is bigger or stronger than the power of God behind you.
Anonymous

DaySpring

Praying that your needs will be met with *God's power* today—and the *love* and *healing* it brings.

And He said to her, "Daughter, your faith has made you well. Go in peace, and be healed of your affliction."
MARK 5:34 NKJV

Perseverance in prayer, a perseverance that strengthens the faith of the believer against everything that may seem opposed to the answer, is a real miracle; it is one of the impenetrable mysteries of the life of faith.

Andrew Murray

DaySpring

Some things in life are hard to undestand. I pray you will feel **God's comfort** today and find ***hope*** and ***faith*** in His ***gentle presence.***

My flesh and my heart may fail,
but God is the strength of my heart
and my portion forever.
PSALM 73:26 NIV

*Life is the question and life is
the answer, and God is
the reason and love is the way.*

Johnny Cash

DaySpring

God makes beautiful things.
I'm trusting Him to
do that for you.

The LORD gives sight to the blind, the LORD lifts up those who are bowed down, the LORD loves the righteous.
PSALM 146:8 NIV

Make each day a masterpiece.
Don't think that your best days are
out there somewhere. Why not today?
Why can't today be a great day?
It can if you believe it will.

John Wooden

DaySpring

God of **compassion** and **mercy,** please reach down and make a way for **healing** and **restoration.**

> "I create the fruit of the lips:
> Peace, peace to him who is
> far off and to him who is near,"
> says the LORD, "and I will heal him."
>
> **ISAIAH 57:19 NKJV**

Our infirmities become the black velvet on which the diamond of God's love glitters all the more brightly.

C. H. Spurgeon

DaySpring

Praying you see how *incredibly valuable you are to God*—that He gives you all you need, every day, to make a difference.

Jesus called His twelve disciples to Him and gave them authority to drive out impure spirits and to heal every disease and sickness.
MATTHEW 10:1 NIV

I used to think that you had to be special for God to use you, but now I know you simply need to say yes.

Bob Goff

DaySpring

The ***joy of Jesus*** is always good news—***healing hearts, changing lives, and creating hope.*** Here's praying that you know ***His joy*** today in all the ways you need.

> Now Jesus began to go all over Galilee, teaching in their synagogues, preaching the good news of the kingdom, and healing every disease and sickness among the people.
> **Matthew 4:23 CSB**

Sometimes the miracle is simply His mercy.
Jane Johnson

DaySpring

Whatever you need, *He is for you today.* Praying you know His *perfect peace* and *healing touch* in deep and wonderful ways.

Take up My yoke and learn from Me, because I am lowly and humble in heart, and you will find rest for your souls.
Matthew 11:29 CSB

If I could hear Christ praying for me in the next room, I would not fear a million enemies. Yet distance makes no difference. He is praying for me.

Robert Murray M'Cheyne

DaySpring

I hope He **_encourages_** your heart today with reminders of how much **_He loves you._**

And wherever He went...
they placed the sick in the marketplaces.
They begged Him to let them touch
even the edge of His cloak, and all
who touched it were healed.

MARK 6:56 NIV

Focus on giants—you stumble.
Focus on God—giants tumble.

Max Lucado

DaySpring

No words I could say would do as much as the prayers I can pray. *Lifting you up to Jesus.*

*This is what the LORD God of
your ancestor David says:
I have heard your prayer;
I have seen your tears.
Look, I will heal you.*
II KINGS 20:5 CSB

Prayer may just be the most powerful tool mankind has.

Ted Dekker

DaySpring

I see you there, **_fighting for your health_** with all you've got. I know God sees too. His **_unfailing love_** will get you through...and I'll be here fighting in prayer for you for as long as you need.

> When Jesus came into Peter's house, He saw Peter's mother-in-law lying in bed with a fever. He touched her hand and the fever left her, and she got up and began to wait on Him.
> **MATTHEW 8:14–15 NIV**

The point of your life is to point to Him. Whatever you are doing, God wants to be glorified, because this whole thing is His.

Francis Chan

DaySpring

Be *encouraged* and *strengthened* by *God's unfailing love.*

My prayers are with you.

Then He touched their eyes and said, "Because of your faith, it will happen." Then their eyes were opened.
MATTHEW 9:29–30 NLT

I believe that, as followers of Christ, we are commanded to reach out to the least of these in the name of Jesus and show them that they matter a great deal to God, who sacrificed His only Son to reach them with His love.

K. P. Yohannan

DaySpring

It may not be clear what He's up to, but I know that **God's plans are good,** and I can't wait to see how it all unfolds in your favor. I hope it helps to know that **you're often in my prayers!**

But for you who fear my name, the sun of righteousness will rise with healing in its wings, and you will go out and playfully jump like calves from the stall.
Malachi 4:2 CSB

Fear not the storm; it brings healing in its wings, and when Jesus is with you in the vessel, the tempest only hastens the ship to its desired haven.
C. H. Spurgeon

DaySpring

Where there's a need for *hope*, *Jesus is there*. Where there's a need for *healing*, *Jesus is there*. Where there's a need for *joy*, *Jesus is there*. Where there's a need for *love*, *Jesus is there*. And I'm praying you feel it all.

"But that you may know that the Son of Man has power on earth to forgive sins"—then He said to the paralytic, "Arise, take up your bed, and go to your house."

MATTHEW 9:6–7 NKJV

Keep this in mind, though: loving people the way Jesus did is always great theology.

Bob Goff

DaySpring

God is **near.**
**Close. Present.
With you always.**
You never have been...
you never are...and
you never will be alone.

The prayer of faith will save the sick person, and the Lord will raise him up; if he has committed sins, he will be forgiven.
JAMES 5:15 CSB

When you understand that God is with you, that changes everything.
Linda Evans Shepherd

DaySpring

Praying that His *healing touch* will *restore you,* His *faithfulness* will keep your heart at *peace,* and His arms will cradle you in *loving care.*

And the Lord will protect you from all sickness.
DEUTERONOMY 7:15 NLT

Everything we take to God—every need, every care, every problem—is never taken in vain. He is forever healing in His own special way and in His own special time.

Anonymous

DaySpring

God is the *Healer*... and *you're in His hands*. Praying for the Lord to fill you with *peace* as He brings *healing* and *comfort* during your hospital stay.

Don't worry about anything, but in everything, through prayer and petition with thanksgiving, present your requests to God. And the peace of God, which surpasses all understanding, will guard your hearts and minds in Christ Jesus.

PHILIPPIANS 4:6–7 CSB

A setback is a setup for a comeback.

T. D. Jakes

DaySpring

Sometimes ***God shows up*** in the most tangible ways we need Him. I've asked Him to be as real to you as ever, through ***hands that heal*** and ***hearts that love.***

Now, Lord…grant to Your servants that with all boldness they may speak Your Word, by stretching out Your hand to heal.
Acts 4:29–30 NKJV

I see the church as a field hospital after battle. It is useless to ask a seriously injured person whether he has high cholesterol and about the level of his blood sugars. You have to heal his wounds. Then we can talk about everything else.
Pope Francis

DaySpring

Thinking of you today.
He will faithfully meet all your needs, He will always be with you, and with Him all things are possible.

Do not be wise in your own eyes; fear the LORD and shun evil. This will bring health to your body and nourishment to your bones.
PROVERBS 3:7–8 NIV

When trouble comes, focus on God's ability to care for you.

Charles Stanley

DaySpring

Asking God to **bless you** with all the things that will assure you of **His love, His presence,** and **His daily care for you.**

God exists and…He rewards those who sincerely seek Him.
HEBREWS 11:6 NLT

Peace is within reach, not for lack of problems, but because of the presence of a sovereign Lord.
Max Lucado

DaySpring

Sometimes God puts just the right *person* in just the right *moment* on just the right *place* of our path. I've asked Him to meet you right there today—through the *love and kindness of others.*

Pleasant words are a honeycomb: sweet to the taste and health to the body.
PROVERBS 16:24 CSB

Far from being a way to achieve success, ease, and comfort, Christianity calls us to live a life that forgets self and focuses on being God's instrument to show His love to others.

Michael W. Smith

DaySpring

For someone who's usually so busy giving your time and energy to **serve others**—having to stay quiet so you can **rest** and **heal** has got to be hard. ***Praying for you!***

> For our light and momentary troubles are achieving for us an eternal glory that far outweighs them all.
> **II Corinthians 4:17 NIV**

Believing that life interruptions—divine interruptions—are a privilege not only causes us to handle them differently but to await them eagerly.

Priscilla Shirer

DaySpring

Praying that God *blesses you* with what only He can give— *deep rest, everlasting peace, and true wisdom.*

The Spirit of the Lord is on Me, because He has anointed Me to proclaim good news to the poor. He has sent me to proclaim freedom for the prisoners and recovery of sight for the blind, to set the oppressed free.
LUKE 4:18 NIV

If you do a good job for others, you heal yourself at the same time, because a dose of joy is a spiritual care.

Dietrich Bonhoeffer

DaySpring

No matter what life may bring you, ***God cares about it all!*** I'm praying for you.

So humble yourselves before God.
James 4:7 NLT

You are a spirit, you have a soul, and you live in a body. You have emotions, you have thoughts, you have a will, and you have a conscience. You are a complex being! And Jesus came to heal every single part of you. There's not one part that He doesn't want to make completely whole.

Joyce Meyer

DaySpring

May Jesus's *healing presence* be *very near* in your time of recovery.

Jesus Christ is the same yesterday, today, and forever.
Hebrews 13:8 CSB

There is no pit so deep that God's love is not deeper still.

Corrie ten Boom

DaySpring

God is in the hard moments with us. **_Even while we're waiting, He's working._** I'm **_waiting, praying,_** and **_believing_** with you.

I have come that they may have life, and that they may have it more abundantly.
JOHN 10:10 NKJV

Never doubt God in the darkness what He has given us in the light.

Francine Rivers

DaySpring

You're surrounded by *caring thoughts today...* and you're in the arms of a *loving, faithful Father.*

Heal the sick who are there and tell them, "The kingdom of God has come near to you."
LUKE 10:9 NIV

For our growth in power and happiness depends upon the number of seconds out of each twenty-four hours that we are resting in God.

Glenn Clark

DaySpring

God's ***tender mercies are new every morning,*** fresh-picked with ***grace,*** fragrant with ***hope,*** and reflecting the quiet beauty of ***His constant love.*** I'm trusting Him to show you His goodness and care as you ***rest in Him.***

> And suddenly, a woman...came from behind and touched the hem of His garment.... Jesus turned around, and when He saw her He said, "Be of good cheer, daughter; your faith has made you well."
>
> **MATTHEW 9:20–22 NKJV**

Lord, enable us to walk as we believe.

Ruth Chou Simons

DaySpring

We have an *awesome God* who is afraid of no storm, who tells waves when to cease, who brings rainbows after rain. I'm trusting Him to *see you through.*

My grace is all you need.
My power works best in weakness.
II Corinthians 12:9 NLT

A healed memory is not a deleted memory. Instead, forgiving what we cannot forget creates a new way to remember. We change the memory of our past into a hope for our future.

Lewis B. Smedes

DaySpring

Lord, someone You love so much is hurting. Draw her ***close to You*** and give her the ***peace*** and ***comfort*** only You can give.

For My yoke is easy and My burden is light.
Matthew 11:30 NKJV

When you accept the fact that sometimes seasons are dry and times are hard and that God is in control of both, you will discover a sense of divine refuge, because the hope then is in God and not in yourself.

Charles Swindoll

DaySpring

I'm asking God to *provide for you* day by day as you trust Him for the *strength and courage* He promises.

Jesus...went about doing good and healing all...because God was with Him.
Acts 10:38 CSB

People pay attention when they see that God actually changes persons and sets them free.

Jim Cymbala

DaySpring

I'm asking God to **bless you with all the good things** He has in His heart for you.

For we walk by faith, not by sight.
II Corinthians 5:7 NKJV

God is loving you into better relationships. He is loving you into being a more loving person. The more we grow in love, the less offended we become. The less offended we become, the more easily and quickly we get healed when people do wound us.

Graham Cooke

DaySpring

I'm sorry you are going through this, but, knowing you, you will be busy showing the world the tough stuff you are made of. *And I'll be praying and cheering you on all the way.*

Now then, stand still and see this great thing the LORD is about to do before your eyes!
I Samuel 12:16 NIV

Stay strong! Your test will become a testimony; your mess will become your message.

Max Lucado

DaySpring

May the God of
***encouragement*…
strength…*healing*…**
send all three to you now.
Encouragement to ***refresh*** you.
Strength to ***renew*** you.
Healing to ***restore*** you.

> The LORD will strengthen him on his bed of illness; You will sustain him on his sickbed.
>
> **PSALM 41:3 NKJV**

God never said that the journey would be easy, but He did say that the arrival would be worthwhile.

Max Lucado

DaySpring

As you go through this challenging time, I'm praying for *comfort, wisdom, and healing* in the tenderest parts of your heart.

He heals the brokenhearted and binds up their wounds.
PSALM 147:3 NIV

Healing is a process we don't have to go through alone. We sometimes think that God isn't working in our lives, but He is, right where we are.

Jennifer Ueckert

DaySpring

When I think of you, I remember someone who is ***bravely fighting*** a hard battle...someone who won't ***give in, give up, or surrender.*** You're a ***warrior and a winner.*** Praying for you.

Faith shows the reality of what we hope for;
it is the evidence of things we cannot see.
Hebrews 11:1 NLT

*God is with me. Jesus is near.
The Spirit is greater than my fear.*
Ted Dekker

DaySpring

I know there's nothing
I can do to make this hard time
go away, but please know
I'm here for you and that
I'm praying every day.

*This is my comfort in my affliction:
Your promise has given me life.*
PSALM 119:50 CSB

The Lord would have us not have the answers, that we might find ourselves wholly submitted to Him, trusting in His care, and dependent on His leading.

Troy Simons

DaySpring

As you're healing...
I'll be kneeling!

They brought to [Jesus] all those who were afflicted, those suffering from various diseases and intense pains, the demon-possessed, the epileptics, and the paralytics. And He healed them.

MATTHEW 4:24 CSB

*God will heal and mend.
It's what He does, it's who He is.*

Kaitlyn Bouchillon

DaySpring

Just thought you should know—you're in *so many prayers that heaven is working overtime!* Keep holding on—or better yet, know that God is right there *holding on to you.*

When Jesus saw her, He called her over and said, "Dear woman, you are healed of your sickness!"
LUKE 13:12 NLT

The high heaven covereth as well tall mountains as small molehills, and mercy can cover all. The more desperate thy disease, the greater is the glory of thy Physician, who hath perfectly cured thee.

Abraham Wright

DaySpring

God will do in your life what only He can do— **strengthen you** with His **love,** fill you with His **assurance,** bless you with His **peace,** and **hold you in His arms** as we hold you in **our prayers.**

In view of God's mercy...offer your bodies as a living sacrifice, holy and pleasing to God—this is your true and proper worship.
ROMANS 12:1 NIV

Where our strength runs out, God's strength begins.

Anonymous

DaySpring

Remembering you in prayer today. I believe that *God's goodness* will cover you *today and always.*

But Peter said [to a lame beggar], "I don't have any silver or gold for you. But I'll give you what I have. In the name of Jesus Christ the Nazarene, get up and walk!"
ACTS 3:6 NLT

God can't give us peace and happiness apart from Himself, because there is no such thing.

C. S. Lewis

DaySpring

Lord Jesus, Your loved one stands in need of healing. Please take away the **pain,** lift this **heavy burden,** and satisfy **each and every need.** Jesus, **bless Your loved one** with a happy heart once more.

And the Lord's healing power was strongly with Jesus.
Luke 5:17 NLT

Tell God what's on your heart, and don't be afraid to pray for those who need healing.
Linda Evans Shepherd

DaySpring

God is at work in ways you can't even *imagine.* Praying you see *His good work very soon.*

> "Lord," the man said, "if You are willing, You can heal me and make me clean." Jesus reached out and touched him. "I am willing," He said. "Be healed!"
>
> MATTHEW 8:2–3 NLT

One day, sweet darling. One day.
There will be no more sickness.
No more death. No more sadness.
We will all be healed.

Beth Moore

DaySpring

***Trusting the God
of every blessing,***

who is good in every way,

to rest His hand upon you and

bring you health today.

My soul, bless the LORD,
and all that is within me,
bless His holy name.
PSALM 103:1 CSB

*No matter what is going on around us,
God is in control. He has not fallen off His throne
and never will. Every moment of our lives is
planned by God. He makes no mistakes.*

Sheila Walsh

DaySpring

I'm praying toward the day when this period in your life will be known not just as that time when hard stuff made your life kind of miserable...but that time when *a seed of hope grew boldly in your heart.*

And He said to her, "Daughter, be of good cheer; your faith has made you well. Go in peace."

Luke 8:48 NKJV

Faith doesn't always mean that God changes your situation. Sometimes it means He changes you.

Steven Furtick Jr.

DaySpring

I'm not in your shoes,
so I won't try to say that I
understand. But I can say
with all my heart that
I will stand with you!

> If you have faith as small as a mustard
> seed, you can say to this mountain,
> "Move from here to there," and it will move.
> Nothing will be impossible for you.
>
> **MATTHEW 17:20 NIV**

*We are all faced with a series
of great opportunities brilliantly
disguised as impossible situations.*

Chuck Swindoll

DaySpring

Turning to God in times of need isn't weakness at all—it's actually the ***strongest thing you can do.*** Praying for you!

So Moses cried out to the LORD, "O God, I beg you, please heal her!"
NUMBERS 12:13 NLT

Having the answers is not essential to living. What is essential is the sense of God's presence during dark seasons of questioning.

Ravi Zacharias

DaySpring

Sometimes life is hard and it hurts. I'm praying for you today and asking Him to ***reassure your heart.***

Then He said to the man, "Stretch out your hand." And he stretched it out, and it was restored as whole as the other.
Matthew 12:13 NKJV

It would be a shame for God to want to do more and for you to settle for less.
Steven Furtick Jr.

DaySpring

Trusting God in *His goodness*
to give you the *strength*
and *courage* you'll need,
every step of the way.

*Therefore we do not lose heart.
Though outwardly we are wasting away, yet
inwardly we are being renewed day by day.*

II Corinthians 4:16 NIV

God searches through our
personal history and heals what
needs to be healed.

Thomas Keating

DaySpring

One day at a time is never easy...but you definitely have what it takes to come through this, ***stronger than ever.***

We also glory in tribulations, knowing that tribulation produces perseverance; and perseverance, character; and character, hope.
ROMANS 5:3-4 NKJV

*Faith does not eliminate questions.
But faith knows where to take them.*

Elisabeth Elliot

DaySpring

I believe in the healing power of *laughter*, of *love*, of *touch*, of *prayer*...and today I'm hoping you will *relax and feel all the love, comfort, and strength* within you and around you.

*In my desperation I prayed,
and the LORD listened;
He saved me from all my troubles.*

PSALM 34:6 NLT

You do not need to understand healing to be healed or to know anything about blessing to be blessed.

Frederick Buechner

DaySpring

Praying you'll be **_refreshed today by God's Spirit_**—the Source and supply of every blessing.

> May the LORD make His face shine on you and be gracious to you; may the LORD look with favor on you and give you peace.
>
> **NUMBERS 6:25–26 CSB**

Hope is placing the beautifully vulnerable parts of ourselves, our raw selves, into His hands. I believe hope moves His heart; but hope also moves our hearts into His hands. Hope builds trust.

Natalie Brenner

DaySpring